The Lost Papers of the Scientific Age

Miguel A. Sanchez-Rey

Table of Contents

To handle a language skillfully is to practice a kind of evocative sorcery.

- Charles Baudelaire

Star Wars is Schizophrenic

Author: Miguel A. Sanchez-Rey

The Star Wars Universe is fraught with schizophrenia. By incorporating elements of mythology and folklore, from both Anglo-American culture and other world cultures, the Star Wars Universe attempts to grapple stern issues that involve regicide, genocide, exploitation and family life. Using elements of science fiction, such as cybernetics, interstellar travel, extraterrestrials and the physics of plasma, to bring to life a vast universe of characters and interwoven plot-lines that attempt to induce cathartic experiences that is, nevertheless, short-live. The Star Wars Universe seemingly introduces, at first, the Jedi Knights whom are task to bring peace and stability to the galaxy -- through diplomacy and the threat of light-sabers.

By painfully exposing a conspiracy to topple the Old Republic, the entire Old Republic succumbs to the empire and young Anakin Skywalker, who is destined to become the one that will bring balance to the force, becomes the ruthless and the evil Darth Vader. Soon it's learned that he has a son name Luke Skywalker and Leia Organa, that along with Chewy and Han Solo, go on a galactic quest to uncover their past and bring stability to the galaxy by destroying the Galactic Empire and overthrowing Emperor Palpatine that sets the stage for the New Republic. Yet eventually the New Republic falls into a crisis between the remnants of the Empire and the New Republic that leads to the final destruction of Coruscant and painful realization of the last Jedi.

Star Wars is schizophrenia that becomes a self-defeating movement of regicide, genocide, exploitation and family life. Where the plot-lines do not come to their logical conclusion and also where much of the Star Wars Universe recycles old plot-lines in an attempt to salvage a galaxy in disarray and mass confusion. The Jedi Knights are wiped out, many lives are lost in a galactic battle for supremacy, and the lead characters are killed of one-by-one in an attempt to further a diminishing story-line by incorporating a flaw sense mythology and folklore.

That is Star Wars is a schizophrenic genre, with enormous depth, but with no end in sight to the original plot-line of regicide, genocide, exploitation and family life. In that manner the Star Wars Universe expanded on the original plot-line of regicide, genocide, exploitation and family life, but succumb to the *final conclusion about the Star Wars genre*: it eventually lost contact with the modern facts of utopian science, cultural studies and anthropology, by incorporating itself and repeating outdated mythological and cultural ideas, in order, to salvage an increasingly questionable plot-line that bears no resemblance to the factual logical internal manifestations of psychological development. Where psychological development comes in different forms that doesn't always involve regicide, genocide, exploitation and family life.

The No-Boundary Proposal in Quantum Space-Time

The Leading Professor Miguel Angel Sanchez-Rey [*The Grandmaster, The Master of Space-Time*]
The Physicalist Program

Abstract

What came before the initial state that led to the inflationary early universe?

March 5th, 2018.

The Hartle and Hawking No-Boundary Proposal states that the universe has no boundary. And that any event in space-time is precluded and surpassed by an earlier event and a future event (and vice versa). That space-time is a quantum state of a vast quantum universe where the wave-function of a quantum state of a universe has larger values and that improbable universes has smaller if zero values. Giving the continuum paradox Minkowski space-time is the sum of the dot-product of two events without end. In which, imaginary time transforms Minkowski space-time into quaternion space-time that contains the cosmological wave-function of an inflationary state of a self-referential quantum universe. Where imaginary time is neither imaginary nor real. But self-reflexive -- in such a way, that space and time is without a boundary or a continuum. Implies quantum space-time is null.

Stephen W. Hawking's Grand Legacy

The Leading Professor Miguel Angel Sanchez-Rey [*The Grandmaster, The Master of Space-Time*]

The Academy of Advance Science and the Technological Sciences

Stephen W. Hawking's -- a world-renowned scientist, physicist, and a prolific author, will be fondly remember for his scientific contributions, for his memorable sense of humor and for his honest public intellectualism (Hawking S. W., A Brief History of Time). Hawking's work on black hole thermodynamics (especially on Hawking radiation, No-Hair theorem, p-branes and the singularity), his support and eventual vindication of the existence of gravitational waves (which was considered Albert Einstein's last prediction that fully substantiated general relativities accuracy at the large-scale), his untiring pursuit of a grand unified theory and quantum geometrodynamics, and his battle with Lou-Gehrig's disease, has define his strength, sincerity and good will (Hawking, The Nature of Space and Time) (Hawking, The Large Scale Structure of Space-Time).

A strength, sincerity and good will that has made a lasting difference in the natural sciences. Propelling Stephen W. Hawking as a world-renowned scientist beloved and admired by many who find

Stephen W. Hawking to be an inspirational celebrity of great character.

Stephen W. Hawking, is nevertheless, an indelible figure but best of all he remains very much a role model for many young scientists and scholars (Hawking S. W., The Universe in a Nutshell).

Having accepted the chair -- The Lucasian Chair of Mathematics at Cambridge University -- Stephen W. Hawking brought clarity and a renewed interest in the sciences (giving his input in many different academic fields, i.e., political science, genetics, space engineering, modern computation, and etc.).

An advocate of catastrophe theory, Hawking's imparted awareness of the perils in artificial intelligence, astrobiology, global warming and mass extinction. He openly fought for an improved invigoration of space exploration (launching Breakthrough Star Shot as a collaborative endeavor to send miniature nanobots to Alpha Centauri) (Hawking S. W., Breakthrough Star Shot, n.d.).

Stephen W. Hawking will surely be miss, and though many renowned physicists has had an opportunity to see and interact with Stephen W. Hawking's, his many publications in quantum cosmology, astronomy, superstrings, M-theory, and popular science has led to productive advances in the physical sciences. Encouraging many to pursue a life of science, scholarship and civil activism (Hawking S. W., *On the Shoulders of Giants*) (Hawking, *...Created The Integers*) (Hawking S. W., *The Grand Design*) (Hawking S. W., *The Large Scale Structure of Space-Time*).

Though a controversial proponent of atheistic thought, Stephen W. Hawking remain a staunch supporter of Humanist ethics and experimental philosophy. And, until his peaceful death (in many ways), unafraid of mortality and/or futility -- Stephen W. Hawking's grand legacy lives on even after Albert Einstein's birthday has already come and gone.

The Grandmaster will continue on.

Bibliography

Hawking, S. W. (Ed.). (n.d.). ...*Created the Integers*. Hawking, S. W. (n.d.). *A Brief History of Time*.

Hawking, S. W. (n.d.). *Breakthrough Star Shot*. Retrieved from

http://www.breakthroughinitiatives.org

Hawking, S. W. (Ed.). (n.d.). *On the Shoulders of Giants*. Hawking, S. W. (n.d.). *The Grand Design*.

Hawking, S. W. (n.d.). *The Large-Scale Structure of Space-Time*. Hawking, S. W. (n.d.). *The Nature of Space and Time*.

Hawking, S. W. (n.d.). *The Universe in a Nutshell*.

Foreword

Stephen William Hawking died of complications to Lou-Gehrig's disease, unexpectedly and peacefully, on Albert Einstein's birthday as of March 14th, 2018. World-renowned physical cosmologist and astronomer -- who spent his early academic career, with Sir. Roger Penrose, pursuing research on black holes and the early universe. Laying out the mechanism of how black holes' form and dissipate, it's thermodynamics, the nature of the singularity, the dynamics of black holes, their role in the early universe and how a deep and profound understanding of the black holes can unlock the nature of space-time, including the grand unified theory and quantum geometrodynamics.

Later work focus on making advances in quantum cosmology. Laying out the implications of the grand design, Hawking's conveyed his resolution to the question of superstrings.

Hawking's first manifested the early stages of motor neuron disease while pursuing graduate studies at Trinity Hall, University of Cambridge. Giving a two-year prognosis of life-expectancy, Hawking's nevertheless continued on and completed his graduate studies to receive his PhD in cosmology. As his disorder further progress, Stephen Hawking's ability to walk, talk and write began to deteriorate. Eventually needing the help of a mechanical wheelchair. Later needing a computer text-to-speech to communicate.

Yet Stephen Hawking found very little ease in taking the chair at the University of Cambridge -- knowing full well, at the time, his limited life-expectancy.

Having accepted the chair, Stephen W. Hawking brought renewed prestige to the Lucasian Professorship but was, in his 30-year tenure, increasingly ridiculed and the subject of trashing by the main-stream press (both for his debilitating illness and careful decision-making). For chairs are dreaded honorships bestow to those with questionable academic merit. Yet Hawking's persevered by bringing unique distinction to the Lucasian Chair of Mathematics at Cambridge University. Upon publication of *A Brief History of Time*, Stephen W. Hawking reach world-wide fame as a public communicator in the sciences.

Pressured to bring more respect to the chair, and the increasing impairment of Lou-Gehrig's disease, Stephen W. Hawking's made compromises as the years went by. And even after retirement, his increasing publications in popular science is testimony to Stephen Hawking's commitment to promote the sciences. While the stigma of suffering from Lou-Gehrig's disease, and his willingness to continue on in taking an active leadership role in the sciences (by making concessions, i.e., making educated bets, increasingly giving preplanned talks -- with questions and answers, for the general public, and using the help of writing and text editors, and other researcher scientists, to complete manuscripts), meant the hardship of being increasingly ridiculed by the mainstream scientific community. Hawking's nevertheless stubbornly persisted until the very end of his life.

For having died a peaceful death is indicative of the grief and pain of being a subject of trashing and laughter, but also the acknowledgement (upon his unexpected passing) that Stephen

William Hawking's will be widely regarded as having gone through a difficult ordeal -- passing away on Albert Einstein's birthday, but having lay out a legacy of genuine scholarship and honest civil activism in the sciences that is indicative in his early, mid and late writing.

Writing that will be seen, in the late century, as the modern classics of world literature for many decades afterwards.

Review, *World on Edge* by Edward S. Casey

The Leading Professor Miguel Angel Sanchez-Rey [*The Grandmaster, The Master of Space-Time*]

The Academy of Advance Science and the Technological Sciences

World is on the edge? For Edward S. Casey, the planet seems to be immersed in edges. But the edge is not too far away. The edge seems to be very much an attractive nuisance that gives false-credence to the concept of edges with limits or even edges with pragmatic continuity.

Even then an individual -- from a phenomenological perspective, can be driven over the edge but no further. The world is at the edge of a super-membrane. But the world is also on the edge of a conceptual breakthrough. A breakthrough that brings edges to the forefront of transcendental nihilism.

Edges that are understood to be nihilistic entities that seem to go beyond edges and boundaries.

And what appears as a planet at the edge is in actual a planet that is non-Euclidean. What seems to be a world at the edge is in fact an over-reaction to a psychotic state. For edges are attractors -- that much can be said is true, but even then they repel when someone falls over the edge.

Yet beneath the edge, the world is desperately contemplating other things. Things that have nothing to do with the invalidity or validity of edges and spaces.

Instead just removing the edge-off makes things much simpler and more clear-cut. For environmentalism doesn't dwell on edges and spaces. Rather it dwells on factual truths that are cognizant of the sciences. And for which the sciences see edges as only a small fact of a larger [classical, mechanical] - universe.

That finding the resolution to a catastrophe is the beginning of the end to an edgy futility.

The World on Edge is the work of a distressing nature. Edges is an adulation of a phenomenological contradiction and not to be construed as an answer to the perils of contemporary history.

Even if edges can tell (this and that) about paintings and cognition, it doesn't seem to be an answer as to what makes paintings more than just cult paintings or what makes cognition more than just the nervous system of a Cheshire cat.

For there is something more to edges than what meets the eyes of a person that witnesses the world at the edge. Yet is a wildly-strong person to be reckon with.

References

Casey, Edward S. *The World on Edge*. Indiana University Press: June 16th, 2017.

The Twelve Monkeys at Stony Brook University

The Leading Professor Miguel Angel Sanchez-Rey [*The Grandmaster*, *The Master of Space-Time*]

The Academy of Advance Science and the Technological Sciences

After the permanent of the decline of the religious state and the sudden breakdown of the Earth's biosphere, the Simons Foundation has then endeavored into political fundraising to cater to their donors and constituency of the Long Island business community. Where in the south shore, organize and gang related crimes have increased and in the north shore, racketeering and higher prices has been an ominous aspect of everyday surrealism. Not too far away is Brookhaven Laboratories and not too close is Cold Spring Harbor Labs (pursuing mediocre and yet cutting-edge experimental science through government and corporate funding).

The Twelve Monkeys at Stony Brook University are cult-figured scientists, pure philosophers and continental theorists. Teaching professors recognized for their achievement in scientific radicalism, radical politics and the fringe literary tradition. They are shunned from much of the mainstream faculty members. Choosing to partake in talks and colloquiums in order to further their agenda for radical transformation of the philosophical sciences, politics and religious transcendentalism.

Ideologically scattered in their visionary aims, they mischievously gather amongst each other to plan out their agenda for world transformation of social norms and taboos. Mildly schizophrenic in their personality types, they preside in their offices as experts in their fields. Meticulously (but benignly in their mannerisms) shuffling their paperwork and filing cabinets, their office hours are split between class discussion and recruitment of students into the army of the Twelve Monkeys.

For the army of the Twelve Monkeys is instrumental in the introduction of cry havoc into the Suffolk County district.

In a matter of eight years, it became a world-wide epidemic of control freaks and thugs.

Where cry havoc can be harness to achieve immediate ends in so little time and cost. But in which in its bio-evolution meant the beginning manifestations of quiet mayhem. An irreversible sociological and anthropological outbreak that has led to lasting damage to the Intergovernmental Panel on Climate Change, the collapse of the global academic hierarchy, and the immediate implementation of a lockdown to contain any further havoc or mayhem. But in which the prize system could not be salvaged, either way.

The original members of the Twelve Monkeys are unknown. But for all intended purposes, one of those members may be affiliated with the Simons Foundation but doubt is cast into the members' motives (and whether or not direct affiliation and/or enrollment is tantamount).

Psychological Assessment: the 12 Monkeys

Deadly teaching and/or research professors (or faculty and/or staff members) involve in radicalism and/or extremist political activism and/or fringe studies. They are usually from affluent and/or privilege backgrounds. Majority wise hold a technical and/or scientific bachelors' degree. Behave like schizophrenics. Shun from most of the faculty members from their prospective university and/or college of employment. And often enjoy causing havoc for their own amusement and enjoyment. Are unaware of the consequentiality of their action and often do not take direct responsibility for any action and/or behavior that may endanger the student population.

The 12 Monkeys are seen as liabilities to the student population. Often encouraging and luring students into atypical behavior that seeks to provoke the student body and/or faculty members into siding with their actions and/or ideology. Can provoke and encourage their students to violently and aggressively misbehave, and often their students begin to maturate psychopathy after prolong provocation and incitement from a 12 Monkey faculty member and/or staff member. 12 Monkeys are by nature reactionary.

Yet hard to spot even with a thorough background check. Usually misconstrued -- as both highly educated and cooperative in temperament, but capable of extreme behavioral tendencies. Nevertheless, carried away by academic life. And usually no sign of a criminal history. 12 Monkey faculty and/or staff member take enjoyment in manipulating others and can often depend on others to meet their superficial needs.

Usually the havoc they cause is organized but unintentional. And often there is money involve with long-term collaboration. Yet very little or no evidence of an attempt to cause intentional harm. But pose an existential threat to long-term harmony in their prospective university and/or college of employment.

Deadly and mildly-psychopathic -- with schizophrenic and predatory aggressive personality type. Silly, benign and mischievous in their mannerisms and behavior, are prone to taking things to the extreme and in causing harm and/or havoc for their amusement. While often manipulating and using others to finance the havoc they cause.

Often by playing games with their students and/or with faculty and/or staff members, etc., etc. Usually a collaborative effort with little or no long-term foresight.

Locally, 12 Monkey -- in dynamics. Globally a cloud-atlas mosaic. A path-psychological (behavioral cognitive and psychoanalytic mapping) approach defines the contemporary assessment of the sociopathic norm. Defining warning of the 12 Monkeys is not to be fooled by immediate perception and/or insubstantial bias.

Where the 12 Monkeys are a substitution for a *conventional mosaic* -- an increasing tendency to the norm. Hence the potentiality for the criminality of the absurd -- the nature of which is the mentality of the herd.

Delirium of the American Presidency

The Leading Professor Miguel Angel Sanchez-Rey [*The Grandmaster, The Master of Space-Time*]

The Academy of Advance Science and the Technological Sciences

There is no telling what the American presidency may mean after the New York Times aftershock editorial of regicide in the White House. Or yet can anyone suppose that former president Barack Obama's, belief in the *transformative moment* is anything but an affirmation of a fraudulent presidency in which the corporate sector has taking over the reins of American political power. There can be no denying -- even then, *of a clear and present danger* evident in the former Vice President Joe Biden's assertion of a renewal of the American spirit, when the U.S. is becoming more of a declining union of states (on the edge of separating from the NATO alliance).

Yet Obama's belief in the benevolence of it, is all telling. For it, is not a shared entity but a possessive entity. And to embody, "it" is to embody a false persona of horror and excitement -- but yet, harmless and benign in its very characteristic and nature. For that persona can be seen in a debating House of Congress or in President Donald Trump's support for far-right wing interests (that are counter to the long-term goals of the corporate sector) but exhibit no immediate difference to American constitutional politics.

The U.S. crumbling state infrastructure cannot explain the need for massive U.S. military spending. 10 years of U.S. cult-decision making has made the American presidency a haven for corporate pensions and dividends. And yet wages have been relatively stagnant -- since the end of the Bretton Woods Foundation, and workers' rights have been curtailed by the money managers of American corporate capitalism.

While contemporary free trade agreements continue to spur massive growth in employment and productivity. Yet recurring trade disputes make such agreements suspect to ultranationalist sentiment. Inciting U.S. isolationism and indifference to international political and corporate interests. But even then, U.S. hegemony remains a key part of its military strategy.

The delirium of the American presidency has been noticeable. What seems as a fanciful posture to invigorate American politics -- is instead, an attempt to revitalize political norms that were place to protect corporate and state power structures that are no longer of any meaningful justification.

The American presidency may seem altruistic and cohesive in its composure. But with varying self-interests, the American presidency makes pragmatic policy-making a demented and delirious enterprise.

Pragmatic policy-making that is the product of atypical decision-making that becomes counter-productive to U.S. long-term strategic and financial interests. But in which such atypical decision-making may manifest itself as corporate short-term gains in U.S. policy-decision making.

Hence solidifying the corporate governorship in return for more executive privilege and power. Igniting a power struggle between varying self-interests -- within the political establishment, in an attempt to shape U.S. politics and its global implications.

A delirious turning point in modern American political history. But in which ultra-nationalist sentiment has eluded to both an irreversible and atypical coup in ideology and praxis. The permanently declining religious state has become a majority consensus not only in contemporary radicalism but in global politics.

No Legislative Power and the Jimmy Carter Era

The Leading Professor Miguel Angel Sanchez-Rey [*The Grandmaster*, *The Master of Space-Time*]

The Academy of Advance Science and the Technological Sciences

The Democratic Party has won the Congressional elections is the hearsay of *The New York Times* at the late-night drama after party. But yet no legislative power is the unanimous decision of the Republican dominated Senate. The democratic party has unleashed the Jimmy Carter era of taking bold and unorthodox risk. And yet they stand to lose everything, either way.

There is near sighted evidence that the Democrats can declare victory in the House of Representatives. With calls for social democracy and a blue wave that crashes into the heart of downtown Republican main street at Washington avenue, but yet the entire democratic party has unexpectedly shot themselves into gridlock and stalemate. Where even the anti-war movement is awestruck by the collapse of the establishment and the solidification of corporate power -- in return, for more executive power and privilege.

But the deal has been called off and the Republicans can now have their last laugh. It ends with a debating house of Congress and it begins with the executive order that solidifies the corporate dominance of the free market, the curtailing of the freedom of speech and the counter-reaction of reporters and the world press that have little say in the affairs of a scientific dictatorship (on the brink of a massive breakdown in the constitutional order through the over-exuberance of social democratic norms). When social democracy has -- either way, met its permanent demise. Yet either way, for the democratic party: it's now the Jimmy Carter era of gridlock and quiet mayhem.

42

The Christmas Eve Before Christmas Day

Today marks Christmas Eve Before Christmas Day. A day that signifies family joining together, the closing of shops and store fronts, the shutdown of government offices and the last-minute effort to give the best Christmas wishes. When happy holidays' is the complement and merry Christmas is the scathing insult.

But Christmas is more than just the utter anticipation of gifts and family gatherings, rather it's the joy of giving and kindness. The act of imparting exemplary acts that make others feel included into the social sphere, while suspending the ideological differences of the political sphere. Either/or, Christmas Eve is a day of anticipating the birth of Christ: it's social and ethical good on phenomenological existence.

As all share an ancestry to Christ birth, and the sanctity of his moral example, more can be done to impart better exemplification. Where acknowledging (the one and the other's) name day can be more genealogically quintessential to the self's relationship to the other -- than the significance of the birth of a religious zealot.

That the birth of a human being, and/or any living entity, is more sacred than the pragmatics of its anthropological-cultural impact. The willingness to accept that horrifying things can potentially occur the day after Christmas morning. And the capacity to empathize with the dire circumstance(s) that makes Christmas into a nightmare after Christmas Day.

Christmas is short-lived. There are better days ahead.

- The Leading Professor Miguel Angel Sanchez-Rey [*The Grandmaster, The Master of Space-Time*]

  at The Academy of Advance Science and the Technological Sciences

The Powerplay of the Radical Democrats

The Leading Professor Miguel Angel Sanchez-Rey [*The Grandmaster, The Master of Space-Time*]

The Academy of Advance Science and the Technological Sciences

Nancy Pelosi's, the House majority leader, and Senator Chuck Schumer open their press conference with a lesson to be learned about legislation.

Even then there is very little legislative potential to be gained that qualifies as political unification across party-lines: congressional deadlock is an evident norm. The contemporary democratic party resorts to impulsive decision-making to incite opposition, but at the expense of radicalizing their base to the near-extent of extreme politics (with little or no direct contact with political reality). Where varying self-interests are motivated by short-term gains.

The winning strategy is for long-term interests to side with short-term gains: to regain control of American political power from radical politics and to pacify the population by implementing *authoritarian practices* meant to subdue impulsive desperation. Radical politics which is based on atypical norms that are on the fringe of economic ideology. Economic ideology that is a byproduct of radical science. Yet transcendentally euphoric in its unreason and political desperation.

Venezuela's Election Crisis

The Leading Professor Miguel Angel Sanchez-Rey [*The Grandmaster, The Master of Space-Time*]

The Academy of Advance Science and the Technological Sciences

The Venezuela crisis is a desperate attempt by the Bolivian revolutionaries to regain control of long-term decision-making. To contain the threat of greater scarcity and rising unemployment cause by years of economic sanctions from the North American Union.

To declare victory in the face of political contradiction, undermines democratic norms. Yet desperate action to maintain socialist ideology -- to sustain civil interests that aim to assert both their cultural heritage and nationalist-aspiration for self-determination, can mean that illegitimate political interests will conspire to undermine an inherently democratic country to regain control of short-term gains (though social democracy has met its permanent demise, international markets are attuned to desperate decision-making on the part of *rogue nations*).

The only avenue is not to condemn desperation, but to address desperate political acts before they solidify into mass-slaughter, conflict and/or war-crime.

Right Decision-Making and Liberal Centrism

The Leading Professor Miguel Angel Sanchez-Rey [*The Grandmaster, The Master of Space-Time*]

The Academy of Advance Science and the Technological Sciences

Hillary Rodham Clinton comes from an affluent background of legal scholarship. A graduate of Yale Law School, Mrs. Clinton has held higher political office since 2001 as New York state senator. Having risen to fame as the First Lady, Clinton rose to power as a high-profile legal scholar (eventually marrying the former president Bill Clinton). As governor of Arkansas, Bill Clinton presided as the key political decision-maker. Battling a slow economy and the emerging neo-conservative wing of the Republican party -- whereby, scandal almost overtook the media limelight.

With growing public approval, the Clintonites set out to win the 1992 American presidency against the 43rd President George W. Bush.

A landslide victory, the Clintonites "transformed" themselves into a transformative democratic couple that revolutionized the edifice of the political process, i.e., through centrism and neo-liberalism. Liberalizing the American economy and relaxing barriers in corporate entrepreneurship, the Clintonites achieved popular policies that led to strong economic growth. Where popularity can invigorate the political process and yet strong decision-making can change the outlook of U.S. power and infrastructure.

Better said, the Clintonites -- though marked by scandal, became a beacon of both progressivism and liberal statism.

Hillary Clinton ran for the 2002 New York state senatorial under the auspices of the Bill Clinton era. Bringing attention to her undying commitment to impoverish groups and to dismantle key Republican policies that favored the super-rich. Using Bill

Clinton's example of centrism through popularity, Hillary Rodham Clinton manage to win the Senatorial race with ease. Yet more ambitious, the Clintonites set out for the 2008 American presidential race.

Running under the ticket of more centrism through popularity, populace politics became center stage in the American pre-election of 2008. The world economy was then struck by a massive housing crisis, yet the Clintonites manage to dissociate from any direct responsibility. Even from Bill Clinton's decision to dismantle the Glass Steagall act that relax banking regulation (implemented during the New Deal).

Either way, the Clintonites sparked mass populist opposition against the Republican party. Populist opposition that proved essential to the Democrats in winning the 2008 elections (using massive funding from the business sector). Also, quintessential to rewarding the private sector that led to the corporate take-over of American political decision-making.

Yet radicalizing their base, Hillary Clinton became Secretary of State under the Barack Obama 2008-2012 presidency -- presiding in key policy-making that altered U.S. foreign affairs and national legislation. Policy-making that is a result of radical maneuvering to invigorate both the Democratic Party and the liberal establishment. Running twice, the Clintonites nevertheless kept their loss in good stride.

Speaking out and reaching out, but keeping a distant watch on the radical transformation of American politics. It's apparent that the Clintonite scandals are an indication of political attempts to evade U.S. legal norms: overreaching decision-making to secure greater political power, using populace politics to steer public opinion against political opponents, and applying unorthodox means to protect their constituency and benefactors. The Clintonites are indicative of populace politics that fails to realize their false promises of progressive change. Instead the Clintonites aspire for more political fame to achieve a Clinton dynasty.

By rewarding the business sector to further intensify failed policy-making -- in an attempt, to secure more presidential privilege. Encouraging a misleading political self-image of liberal centrism. It appears, nonetheless, that Hillary Clinton is a *Palpatine political figure* whose motives are unclear. Yet driven by populace rhetoric and manipulation of key-players -- in an attempt, to present herself as a figure-head that will heed the desperation of the masses by delegitimizing a debating Congress. Pose policy-recommendations meant for their business benefactors that spearheaded her rise to fame and popularity.

Using contemporary trends to claim progressive decision-making -- in hopes, of greater political power to invigorate a misleading and yet declining self-image of liberal centrism.

The American-Zealot

The Leading Professor Miguel Angel Sanchez-Rey [*The Grandmaster, The Master of Space-Time*]

The Academy of Advance Science and the Technological Sciences

Former vice President Joe Biden's tone is zealotry: pronouncements of religious adherence and his admiration for American-patriotism, the liberal demigod is forefront to run for the American presidential office of 2020-2024. Yet admired for his Freudian slips and his demeanor as an honest party democrat, the two party American political system remains in deadlock.

The current President Trump is poise to counter Biden with assertions of Barack Obama's fraudulent presidency of cult-decision making. Even then the breakdown in American politics, of monumental racism and white nationalism in the South, is not enough to solidify Biden's win. World-wide, neo-expansionary politics makes it even more a complicated matter as to whether Joe Biden can sustain party-unity and the genuineness of the democratic party. To the extent that he can preserve U.S. dominance of global politics and international markets.

Yet inherently a centrist liberal, Joe Biden remains trapped within the two-party psyche of American establishment politics. Devoid of any knowledge of the dystopic reality of contemporary social and economic culture. Willing to go along with the radical fringe of the party-democrats. Even capable of taking extreme executive action to realize ulterior ends for purposes of publicity.

An imperialist in his incapacity to even acknowledge the economic and military interest of other world leaders -- whom feel differently about the American corporate governance of the free-market and geo-politics. It seems nothing much has changed in Biden; besides careful-scrutiny of a dubious political campaign. A monumental initiative that will be undertaking by both the business and government sector: whether Biden will reward or punish private interest, even if it meant sacrificing the lower spectrum of American class-ridden consciousness.

It's good riddance to Joe Biden.

The Ancient Philosophers

There is no telling what the philosophical sciences might mean for the contemporary political philosopher, though we all fantasize about the ideal: we must not forget to remind ourselves about the prospect of the Platonic ideal. Many phenomenologists have noted that the ideal is a figment of the chemistry of the brain. Though the ideal is also a mathematical formulation, truth is much more conducive than factuality. Even as the sciences are factual constructs of metaphysical idealism. It's one thing to fantasize about the ideal utopian state, it's another to be honest if the ideal utopian state obligates to all our notions about physical reality: laws of nature and natural principles, that are the bedrock of modern philosophy of science.

I suspect much of the faculty members have a social tendency to fantasize about their self-image and being, "authority figures" in the limelight of cult-figure status. Instead, what you observe is the frail nature of their limited inhibitions to make proper and effective use of their tenure as academics and intellectuals. They pose themselves as gatekeepers to elite decision-making, instead they're rudimentary philosophers giving the humane provocative to publish and instruct for absolutely no purpose besides for the fun of it.

My own views of my former teachers in philosophy, is that they be inclined to do low things (even in the eyes of a renowned philosopher). They made their own decision to commit dishonest acts in academia, yet they are undoubtedly non-pedantic about it. Extremists involved in radical philosophy. And yet immeasurable to a mature outlook on contemporary civility. Barbaric in their philosophical ideology, but too fixated on neo-Fascist sentimentality.

The faculty members in philosophy are disturbed in their collective consciousness, especially in their preconceptions of philosophical truth-values. And what values are those are unknown to even a Greek sophist. There is nothing more to be said, besides their pointless in their motives and yet absurd in their theatrics: reflecting a haunting self-image of passive criminality, very much like a satanic cult. In which they increasingly swarm in and eventually devour their (student)s in a deadly game of merry-go-round, before even their own (student)s realize the full extent of their involvement in their academic outcome.

- The Leading Professor Miguel Angel Sanchez-Rey [*The Grandmaster, The Master of Space-Time*]

at The Academy of Advance Science and the Technological Sciences

On the Democratic Party on Both Ends

The Leading Professor Miguel Angel Sanchez-Rey [*The Grandmaster, The Master of Space-Time*]

The Academy of Advance Science and the Technological Sciences

The democratic party establishment is desperate to solidify their grip on congressional and executive power. Yet there is no sign of a democratic leader that can win over most disenfranchised and impoverished Americans -- besides a shattered two-party system on the fringe of political extremism. While democrats resort to defamation to prove political credibility and center-democrats utilize haywire decision-making to sustain their party-base, there is no telling that party-politics is all about being the popularity of the business class. And yet while the elderly statesman, former Vice President Joe Biden, claims that the poet-laureate is a dream come true and while plans are out there for Elizabeth Warren, President Donald Trump is making popular decision-making that brings wild-enthusiasm to the American corporate sector. Reality sets in: it's not going to happen, for they are really that bad.

It's over for the American landscape, in that the edifice of the political establishment collapsed over-night after the first primary democratic debates. In that it appears that none carries the competence to face the factuality of the matter: their political careers are at stake and yet it's a global effort.

And so, the United States goes its separate ways, while the modern world is awestruck by how of a rogue nation the U.S. is becoming, as it gets closer to the 2020 American Presidential elections. Revealing the democratic contenders, for the 2020-2024 American Presidential office, as one the most frightening candidates in global history to have presided in the national media and on the international stage.

In that it was all an act: out of desperation and sheer political incompetence.

Krugmanomics Doesn't Check Out

The Leading Professor Miguel Angel Sanchez-Rey [*The Grandmaster, The Master of Space-Time*]

The Academy of Advance Science and the Technological Sciences

Krugmanomics is the study of Paul Krugman's economic contributions and public intellectualism: new trade theory, new economic geography, and his many articles to the NY Times editorial page that have continued to ascertain contemporary political and economic policy-making. His liberal economics, guided by New Keynesianism, has, for more than two decades -- in which, Krugman has produced results adequate with accepted international trade policy. That said, the demise of social democratic norms has rendered John Maynard Keynes contributions to macroeconomic theory relatively intact, yet economic certainty is no longer a guaranteed certainty.

Instead, liberal and/or conservative politics has become increasingly radicalize to the extent that support for anti-trade and protectionist policies is becoming a more ominous reality. Causing Paul Krugman's models to become more unstable. Instability precipitated by the permanent decline of the United States (U.S.) Federal Reserve, including the World Bank, i.e., primarily produced by the U.S. decision to amend the North Atlantic Free Trade Agreement, which has managed the international markets, i.e., including the then expansionary European common market; founded in the late-1950's, the Bretton Woods Foundation (dismantled in the early-1970's): setting the stage for global free trade and 1980's Reaganomics of cut-backs in social spending, increasing military spending, and unjustifiable economic deregulation – yet putting an end to the unstable usage of the gold standard in inflationary and/or deflationary policy.

Paul Krugman's own contributions to political science has dealt too-many unfortunate setbacks cause by his over-exuberance of left-wing radical politics. Even more, none of his work and perspectives on public intellectualism has produced substantial results.

Results that'll achieve long-term success for the liberal democratic establishment. His advocacy of liberal politics is genuine, but his praxis borders to the extreme of political theory. His inability to hold a centrist stance, has made Krugmanomics into a potentially long abandoned specialized field of modern economic theory. Yet a disturbing trend cause by the increasing profiteering and exploitation of Krugmanomics by fringe groups and cult-figures.

Though revered and highly respected, even amongst the Council of Economic Advisors, Krugman has played a secondary role in economics and has neither achieved the connotation of a renowned expert indicative of an international economist (as the late John Maynard Keynes, the late Paul Samuelson, or even Stanley Fischer). Though Keynesian and genuine in his conscientious liberalism, Paul Krugman is becoming an increasingly forgotten economist and political commentator for the New York Times: a declining global figure that has spark enormous controversy over his columns and policy decision making. But is very much an admired macroeconomist in the contemporary field of New Keynesianism, policy making, modern political science, and the history of the United States civil war. Yet shows potential to become an influential global figure, if both less frantic and more alienated from radical left-wing politics, i.e., which has rendered considerable damage to his reputation; including, the notoriety of the NY Times. But very much, as today, outspoken about liberal causes, human rights and decency; essential to civilized society and progressive politics.

Either way, Krugmanomics doesn't check out but only time will tell -- if Krugmanomics regains its noticeable promise as long as adjustments are made to his trade models and economic policy making. More of an outspoken dissident. Less frantic in his literary style. And dissociated from fringe groups and cult-figures, especially the far-left wing of the democratic establishment, i.e., Alexandria Ocasio-Cortez, Bernie Sanders, etc., etc.

The Split-Collective Consciousness of the Contemporary Modernist Dystopian Reality

The Leading Professor Miguel Angel Sanchez-Rey [*The Grandmaster, The Master of Space-Time*]

The Academy of Advance Science and the Technology Sciences

The planetary collective mind has gone into a split state -- in which, the human psychological consciousness has lost contact with the condition and perils of the biosphere. Whereby the global psyche -- seemingly non-abstruse and cordial, is instead agitated and profoundly confused.

Below the horizon is mass social unrest and the potentiality for violent predisposition that risk to break the treatises of the sovereign nations of the developing world. What may seem as a planet in recovery from decades of economic plight, is nonetheless the rising force of a dynasty class. Those who take part in elite decision-making recognizes the contributions of a modernist thinker, yet are unaware of the horrific consequentiality of their own tendency to produce banal decisions. Taking part in historicism; aloof to the troubling circumstances of their absurd-consciousness.

The split-collective psyche is indicative of a macrocosm that cannot -- in any factual formulation, distinguish between a modernist dystopia and a utopian paradise. Instead carelessly wander about its internal consciousness, unaware of the horrid outcome of their atypicality.

That said, the population, within the northern western hemisphere -- in a split-identity conscious (instigated by the supreme racism that antagonized the other), is adamant to confront the differences of factuality. Rather the population chooses to go about their daily lives without aforementioned foresight. Yet the more the collective-psyche splits, the potentiality for catastrophic exponential violence and mass revolt becomes a tantamount realism of the modern industrialized and developing countries.

In consequence, the contemporary modernist dystopian reality has observed the collective-psyche split into a preconditional awareness of unrealism. Where paradise lost is unrecognizable, even to an advocate of peace-time. Yet nations are bewitched by totalitarian policies masquerading as democratic movements. And the scientific process is now confronted by a burgeoning crisis of unconscious acts of growing self-violence and deluded indistinguishability of bewitchments.

Ominous American Presidential Election at the Scientific Age

The Leading Professor Miguel Angel Sanchez-Rey [*The Grandmaster, The Master of Space-Time*]

The Academy of Advance Science and the Technological Sciences

Former Vice President Joe Biden steps into the election defending his actions and policies with passionate charisma, while Elizabeth Warren pleads sense with logical circularity. President Donald Trump haywire decision-making subsides with the threat of impeachment and the growing accusation by the House Democrats, including Nancy Pelosi, even former Vice President Joe Biden, of violating the U.S. (United States) Constitution barring foreign intervention.

The democratic race is one of passion and intuitionist logic. Where the presidential candidates sort out the logical observation of the nature of American and global politics, to assess their own moral intuitions.

There is no conspicuousness that desperation is subsiding, but all presidential candidates split-mindedness dictates a divided and heated presidential race with differing socio-ideological outlooks. In equal remark, the Republicans remain diffident and quietly reserved. Yet steadfastly confrontational of Joe Biden; including, Senator Bernie

Sanders socialist stance; though social democratic norms have met its permanent demise. There are grounds for mistrust, but prevailing historical policy has led to decision-making that has no bearing to America's global stature -- though a largely state-capitalist economy that drives international capital and trade.

Ominous as it seems, the candidates are split, more than divided about their earlier decision-making; yet too contingent on their sensibility of character.

Posing accusations of failed policies to Joe Biden, and similarly hypocritical and confrontational claims of misinformation toward the U.S. democratic candidates -- directed by Joe Biden. Where the public is unable to reconcile the candidates, instead they waiver toward the Republican ideological stance. Either sedentary or radically wistful of the 2020 American presidential elections. To the intensity that all candidates bear no difference to contemporary American politics.

Test Model for One of the Most Frightening Universities in Global History

The Leading Professor Miguel Angel Sanchez-Rey [*The Grandmaster, The Master of Space-Time*]

The Academy of Advance Science and the Technological Sciences

Stony Brook University (SBU), base at Suffolk County, New York, presents a particular dilemma for higher education: whether Stony Brook is a factual leader in the sciences and arts, and whether or not the University of Stony Brook is the leading public university in the United States (US).

There is this sense that the State University of New York (or SUNY) was founded to provide higher education at a low cost. Giving a presume wealth of opportunities to low-income students, from less affluent academic backgrounds, to pursue a world class education. Yet in the last 17 years, the University of Stony Brook has been besieged by allegations, scandal, higher unemployment, and a county that has falling victim to a health care system that has adopted extreme tactics to cater to more privilege interests; which has led to disproportionality that has greatly affected those of low-income and in poverty.

The modernist architecture and setting of SBU is one of wonder; whereby, first year undergraduates are awestruck by SBU's vast variety of food, recreation, health and counseling services, that has giving the

University of Stony Brook the eloquence of a first-class university within a college system that is confronted by increasing tuition and food prices, and a US academic standard that has seen the dismantling of the core guidelines of the Educational Opportunities Program -- falsely connotating it's summer program as a reputable academy to incoming students, and cuts in funding for the social sciences and the arts. All indicative of a public education centralism that aims to incur massive profits to fuel a county-scale economy, and to integrate with other universities to claim the standing of a global leader in higher education; next only to both Berkeley and Rutgers University.

Having hired world-class teaching professors to instruct their students in higher education, while pursuing research for humane purposes. The University of Stony Brook has gained the notoriety of a cult-university that has been declining since, at its height, of the fall semester of 2002. When the noted scholar, Shirley Strum Kenny, was elected to overhaul Stony Brook's crude education and extensive landscape, to reinvigorate public education. Yet with a world economy at the brink of a housing and banking crises, SBU, by the late-2008, was confronted by massive college debt, and higher food and real estate prices, which greatly affected college well-being; even amongst their faculty and staff.

The noted scholar, Shirley Strum Kenney, eventual retirement, made way for Samuel Stanley to take the reign as president of SBU. With a growing reputation as a world-class public university -- using massive funding, increase taxes, heavy relocation of less affluent groups to make way for the privatization of the north shore, of Suffolk County, Stanley's willingness to take part with the corporate sector, cause SBU to succumb to corrupt interest. Imposing business tactics to employ global cult-figures, as faculty members, to bring prestige to its research department as a long-term investment for public education. Fueling the Long Island economy as a waypoint that sought to take part in elite decision-making, as, "an elite institution, but not an elitist" aiming to infringe on the elite colleges and elite decision-making to make questionable headway, i.e., in its attempt to allow the business class to take over the New York state public education system. In which, the stakes were high to implement its faculty members to promote Stony Brook, but in which radical extremism, amongst its activists and political leadership, enabled for the radicalization of the corporate sector and encouraged the faculty to apply extreme tactics to realize their own radical ends of higher education, counterintuitive, to a humane and welcoming university.

Rather Stony Brook University became a center for state privatization, political mishandling, and corporate-state policies at the borderline of neo-Fascist policies meant to discipline their students to obey an educational institution desperate to become a global leader in higher education. Though, in contradiction, becoming a university that has met its ultimate decline; in the formulation, of having to award honorary doctorates to declining figures, i.e., the Nobel laureate Bob Dylan, the actor, Alan Ada, and the long-time New York State Senator

Chuck Schumer, etc., to pacify their summer graduating class. With notable alumni that has not reach the limelight of historical achievement.

A horrific academic institution, first established as Oyster Bay College, that prides itself as world class, yet deluded enough not to realize it's stature as a public academia that infringes into elite decision making to safe-guard a regional economy, allying with fanatical foundations, i.e., the Simons Foundation, the Templeton Foundation, etc., to increasingly infringe in the elite colleges. Causing Stony Brook University to overexpose its core educational practices, extreme tactics, and cult-figured professors, to the global mainstream media. Resulting in the mainstream media's decision to punish the SUNY public education system with a blackout and fire-wall -- creating, "cult-central" in the Suffolk County district; teeming with corruption and an unprecedented criminal-activity of academic and humanitarian fraudulence.

Becoming a test model for one of the most frightening universities in global history. Both for its brutality and willingness to make ostracism into a planetary normalcy. Yet for its capability for horrid academic policies that tolerates Fascism -- in the modern formalism of neo-Fascist sentiment, to solidify conformity of faculty, staff, and students. Leading to a cascading effect of deadly tactics and norms that could potentially incline itself to totalitarian acts of supreme racism and academic genocide.

The Split-Collective Psychotropic State

The Leading Professor Miguel Angel Sanchez-Rey [*The Grandmaster, The Master of Space-Time*]

The Academy of Advance Science and the Technological Sciences

Transcendentalism nihilism means that there is no more to transcendentalism than existential nihilism. Whereby the manifestation of the life-world is a meaningless void that encompasses the phenomenological state of awareness of non-being. And if wild being is to surpass non-being, then the split-cognitive mindset of disinterest of the causal and moral consequences of non-beings (Dasein) decisions and/or actions must reintegrate to regain temporal existentiality. When the bourgeoisie makes decision making that has consequentiality to the workers of production, there awakens a moment of sense when the bourgeoise fears the revolt of the masses. But when the architectures of industrial production surpass the workers in power, wealth, and privilege, then there is no use to consider the plight of their employees. Rather sit pensively attending to family and close friends on the dinner table, while unaware that the biosphere is eroding into a decaying planet of dead trees and rotting cityscapes.

The horrors of the split-collective state are that not much is said and/or realized, instead the cause of split-decision making -- to implement one and/or two choices splits into multiple acts of absurd and criminal decision making that results into atypical catastrophe. In that, the psychological state of split-conscious is a psychotropic manifestation; consistent with the beneficial outcome of short-term wealth, power, and privilege. Any absurd criminality that succumbs into a split-collective state, is a non-Dasein that is maniacal in its incapacity to make logical intuitionist sense of difference but aims to tear apart difference so as to hide its motive to devour difference to achieve a conclusive role within a varied group.

To solidify its conclusive role within such group structure, is to assume that consequentiality is not an effect of his and/or her own action; for there are practical limits to social and financial conventionality that out way all mismanaged power structures. Yet consequentiality is not to be taken for granted; humans are innately moral non-Dasein's: capable of recognizing biological boundaries and parameters.

For others are bound to become aware of non-Dasein's capabilities; to then rip apart Dasein if there are any subtle difference to what it assumes to be a benign demeanor and a threatening composure to avoid the group-normalcy. Competition amongst groups are motivated by selfish drives for reproduction, but epigenetically, those drives to extend the life-span of the gene carrier persist as the ability to adapt to near perfect decision making that avoids long-term futility; where wild-being far surpasses non-Dasein, i.e., non-being in a psychotropic state of perturb disinterest and anxious dissatisfaction on the borderline of cognitive hysteria.

Non-Dasein is inadequate to confront hysterical cognition. While wild being has nothing to lose in the game of life, then to achieve near-perfect perpetuation of existentiality by acknowledging the others futility -- the essence of nihilistic transcendentalism.

The Day the U.S. Stood Still at the Hill

The Democratic Party, along with the Republican Party, debate at the House of Representatives the articles of impeachment; meant to put an end to almost four years of questionable and corrupt decision making. Where the liberal establishment will be able to move America forward into the 2020 American presidential race; with some sense of contentment.

Even as Donald Trump defends his tenure, the house leader desperately conveys her support to have President Donald Trump remove from higher office and to bring the political establishment into a new era of American liberal politics; where blue-wave fantasy overtakes the United States by storm; regaining its stature as a global military power, i.e., especially, at the forefront of economic leadership. Restoring the U.S. (United States) support for intergovernmental cooperation by revitalizing globalization; propelling the European member states to regain their self-image. In which, the U.S. will set out to promote democracy by rooting out third world leaders who oppose the corporate model.

Either way, it's a huge lost for both the Democrats and the Republicans. Even as behind the scenes; there are talks of resignations and court sentences, the Democratic Party must contend with a bitter 2020 American Presidential Election; where massive funding will likely sway in favor of the corporate money managers. Though House Majority Leader, Nancy Pelosi, received a majority of the vote to begin the impeachment proceedings at the Senate, the corporate-sector grapples with establishing a charismatic Presidential Republican candidate that will motivate their constituency to slaughter the party- Democrats in the 2020 United States elections. Yet incited by President Donald Trump's (potential) resignation -- with long-term repercussions that may lead to severe political retaliation, will only encourage their base to suppress progressive policies and to antagonize progressive liberalism. Most importantly, driven by a corporate model that knows no end; besides the U.S. Supreme Court. And yet with no end in sight.

When the *right thing to do* is to vote Donald Trump completely out of office, rather than have the Democratic Party make an example of the American corporate establishment. Knowing that the corporate sector is playing an increasingly expansionary role in funding the U.S. elections.

Even then a liberal United States Supreme Court is currently non-existent. Whether it to be the former Justice Anthony Kennedy, or any Associate Justice, the swing vote isn't an adequate method to long-term constitutionality. In any case, the corporate model predominates.

- The Leading Professor Miguel Angel Sanchez-Rey [*The Grandmaster, The Master of Space-Time*]

at The Academy of Advance Science and the Technological Sciences

Response to the Postmodernisms' of the Age: Contemporary Issues of Notability

Leading Professor Miguel Angel Sanchez-Rey
The Academy of Advance Science and the Technological Sciences

Postmodernisms' of the Age is a contemporary issue of notability. Though I suspect there are grounds for serious skepticism of what Postmodernisms' entails for humanist philosophy, i.e., the post-modern condition, whether "postmodernisms" is in the stages of its own realization of a transcendental philosophy. Yes, it truly is the end of ideologism; that much is true, for "ideologism" comes in many different formalities; it just isn't about notability, it's about whether the human condition can surpass metaphysical epistemology?

That's why post-modernity attained the information age, because the human condition implies that it encroached into the expert sciences to dwell on political and economic history. That is, to establish a spirit of the age that isn't happening; besides the output is a psychotropic state that took half a year to recover from.

In which, the expert sciences are no longer willing to take part in public intellectualism. Instead, what you see is transcendentalist philosophers and continental philosophers asserting their own "post-modern condition." But yet they claim no affiliation with humanistic psychology; instead what you observe is deluded thinking that doesn't make sense to a Freudian psychoanalyst. Since factuality sets in, there is really no sense to what you or I are saying, if it isn't for a human condition which is radically empiricist and yet not so much an end to history, but the recognition of one's own futility.

Sociology in a Modernist Dystopian Reality

The Leading Professor Miguel Angel Sanchez-Rey [*The Grandmaster, The Master of Space-Time*]

The Academy of Advance Science and the Technological Sciences
The North Atlantic Treaty Organization

The norms of human and/or biological sociology has entered into neurasthenia; with the biosphere reaching a climate breaking point and the rapid loss of biodiversity; human civilization must confront a deadly norm of anti-social conventionality between the pressures of the biosphere and the long-term gains consistent with economic demand -- placing enormous pressure on bioorganic life to compete. Yet the norms of sociological convention are contingent on biological evolutionary adaptation, but also on cultural pragmatics and scientific philosophy.

Thus, the political spectrum; immersed on radical ideology; seeks to tear apart those conventionality to achieve radical ends. Radical ends that are either of a scientific and/or political nature; but unorthodox to the academic order. Yet the struggle for competing ideologies and a planetary system in social disarray; from a psychotropic state, implies that the legal system has not adequately confronted the norm. For those reasons, the planet has entered a sociological state of neurasthenia; where all norms of social convention breakdown to the extent that a dissolution in communal behavior begins to manifest. Where what is indicative as neurosis; is instead, the human consciousness tearing apart its own inhibitions to escape its own futility: to reveal a deadly state of mind; the pure id that auto- immunes the unconscious; awakening the human mind into a wonderland far lost; but shattered by its own radical consciousness.

To break through a defense firewall, the norm has torn apart the psyche of the biosphere; to achieve ulterior ends; by using its false association with the other to justify its existentiality. Not realizing the deadly aspect of what the norm was asking for; the permanent collapse of contemporary biological sociology.

94

The Matrix is Done
Leading Professor Miguel Angel Sanchez-Rey

The Matrix is a science-fiction and/or fantasy trilogy; and/or contemporary saga, that test the boundaries of filmography and transcendental politics; the pinnacle of the golden age of post-modernism, the search for the one that will defeat the machines and allow Zion to realize its nationalist goals for independence. A computerized holographic mainframe design to control the human population, most of the Matrix human inhabitants are unaware that they are enslaved as batteries; fueling the energy needs of the artificial superintelligent (super-A.I.) machines that dominate a scourging and dying planet.

Mr. Thomas A. Anderson is a computer programmer living a double life; as an underachieving software developer and as a black-market pirate. At the height of 1990's era Mega City; Mr. Anderson follows a white rabbit mark; to encounter Trinity and then Morpheus.

Led down the rabbit hole by Morpheus; between either the blue pill or the red pill, Neo confronts Zion's war with the machines and their struggle for liberation. Neo meets the Oracle and confronts many other key characters; pushing the boundaries of the norms of transcendentalism and contemporary politics -- within a paranoid and euphoric non-factuality of existentiality.

Confronting themes of domination, imperialism, and colonialism, especially the psychology of sexuality, the state, and polity, the Matrix becomes an experience machine that achieves transcendentalist sadism through a misinformed catharism. But when all is said and done, the Oracle fails to tell Neo what the Oracle knows all too well: his career as a software developer is done; yet it just wasn't enough. Instead, Neo, persist in his involvement with the wrong influence; to wake up as far more than a software developer; rather as a split-minded psychological ontology.

In which, Neo can't distinguish between the specialized knowledge of foundational epistemology and computer holography. Instead, sets out to justify extreme tactics of warfare and violence to achieve radical ends of liberation theology; to reach a transcendental post-modernism in an irreversible hell on Earth. Yet willing to independently co-exist with a machine superintelligence which is far more advanced than the human biological form.

When the best interest is to integrate their biology with the super-A.I. machines, rather than to prolong independent co-exist. As conflict is an imminent factor between an ostracize intelligence and a superintelligence which must contend with a primitive race on par with a domesticated animal, i.e., the only resolution -- between warfare and lasting peace, is to abandon Zion's militaristic and terror policies; to accept the sovereign authority of the machines by the implementation of human cybernetics. To accomplish mutual goals of cooperation for lasting tranquility, rather than a formulation of self-interest that risk to ignite a more catastrophic conflict that could tear apart the very fabric of theoretical realism.

The Oracle is so dead, Neo's career is done. And we'll only know when the day comes. When it never happened, for it just wasn't enough. And so, he shot himself; the prescribed horror of a twisted saga.

Anticipatory Market Fluctuations as an Imminent Threat to the International Markets

Dr. Miguel Angel Sanchez-Rey, The Leading Professor
The Academy of Advance Science and the Technological Sciences

Markets, from the Tokyo Stock Exchange to Wall Street, are rattling themselves with the highest anticipation of a stimulus package on steroids. With checks waiting to be shipped out to millions of Americans, and with direct deposits aiming to be cleared by the Bank of America for thousands of middle income home owners, an American economy with a no-win of either COVID- 19 related food illnesses, COVID-19 breakouts across million dollar malls, and the lack of inventory (due to store closures and chapter-11's -- by Nigerian scam agencies housing thousands of low income Americans); the threat that there's nothing there but a black Friday sale that ends in a screaming fight for a finite amount of rations and food pantries. It's all an indicator that the millions of checks and direct deposits which are being distributed by the United States (U.S.) Treasury are *dead on arrival*.

Meaning that millions of shoppers (whether retail, online, or small-business) have been sent to their screaming death with worthless checks that will take days, if not weeks, to spend. Causing the international markets to rattle and fluctuate to the point of a global catastrophic failure in liquidity (between supply and/or demand).

It's Sodom and Gomorrah on U.S. soil.

Institute for Advanced Study (IAS): A Haven for Crackpottery

Dr. Miguel Angel Sanchez-Rey, The Leading Professor
The Academy of Advance Science and the Technological Sciences

The Institute for Advanced Study (IAS) is a private academic institution meant to pursue further studies in all areas of higher education. Founded in 1933, the IAS, located at Princeton, New Jersey, in the United States (U.S.), invited promising researchers and academics from all walks of life -- in higher education, to advance the institutes mission of producing world-leaders in the sciences through a self-disciplinary process of academic learning, i.e., by way, of an interactive process of pacification with world renowned faculty members and experts.

Fostering cooperation between the private sector and higher education; promoting American science and corporate entrepreneurship. Using their endowment and funding to spearhead the institutes role as a global leadership in cutting edge sabbaticals, lectures, membership, and fellowships; inaugurating continuing high achievement and groundbreaking research.

The Institute for Advanced Study, first tenured by non-other than Albert Einstein, Kurt Gödel, John Von Neumann; have included in the modernist era, such leading figures as Edward Witten, the late Freeman Dyson, and as a non-tenured faculty member, the late John Nash. Many mathematical figures, John Milnor, Robert P. Langlands, Michael Atiyah, and Alonzo Church (the noted logician) have presided at the institute as faculty and invited members -- later gaining notoriety and renowned recognition in pure mathematics. The School of the Social Sciences, at the IAS, have also garnered notable but controversial scholars: Rebecca Newberger Goldstein (philosopher and novelist), Patricia Churchland (self-proclaimed neurophilosopher from the Santa Fe Institute, California), Michael Walzer, etc.

The IAS, since its founding, has housed the leaders of the academic world as a haven of promising scholarship. But much of the academic leadership that were invited to the institute -- eventually assuming faculty positions at the IAS -- defied the American liberal centrist-order through radical ideological viewpoints in their prospective field: a primary decision factor for invitation to the IAS; aiming to accelerate the U.S. international dominance of the competitive sciences (by extremizing the academic intelligentsia).

To spur interest in the institute through unorthodox research -- posing themselves as world leaders -- instead, produce crackpottery that eventually backfired on the American scientific establishment and much of the United States educational system.

Albert Einstein invitation to the institute, under the auspices of world fame and a controversial 1921 Nobel Prize in Physics (for the photoelectric effect); instead, his career concludes after the Copenhagen dispute with Niels Bohr. Deduced by the world press as unbecoming of a global leader of his academic stature, Albert Einstein is suggestive of early signs of schizophrenia that manifest itself as a zealous enthusiasm for crackpottery that eventually morphed into radical research after arriving at the IAS. Even then, the IAS has introduced faculty members and invited scholars considered to be overly-qualified; especially:

Kurt Gödel and Rebecca Newberger Goldstein; in the production, of derogatory research and pointless literary works; both respectively. Especially, John Milnor's 2011 Abel Prize fiasco and Edward Witten's published papers, on the string interactions, that infer premature claims of a theory of everything in the world press during the 2014 Kyoto Prize.

Engulfing the entire IAS at Princeton, New Jersey into scientific radicalism -- by excessive and unprecedented undertakings of increasingly wide-spread academic fraudulence, ideological fanaticism, and impetuous publicity through over-indulgence. With the IAS core research areas having no added bases in the experimental sciences; yet encouraged by risky private donations and corporate funding (the Templeton Foundation, the Simons Foundation, etc.), e.g., Freeman Dyson and Robert P. Langlands. Bringing in more faculty members and visitors from the fringe of academic scholarship, e.g., Nima Arkani-Hamed and Cumrun Vafa -- in a desperate attempt to outcompete in an increasingly global academia that is becoming more suspicious of the IAS.

Instead, the IAS prevails as a haven for crackpottery which concludes with a nation-wide breakdown in American higher education and scholarship.

Pillage and Plunder Do America

Dr. Miguel Angel Sanchez-Rey, The Leading Professor
The Grandmaster, The Master of Space-Time
Doctor of Non-Theoretic (Nt.d)
The Academy of Advance Science and the Technological Sciences

The pillage and plunder of the United States (U.S.) Treasury emphasizes the desperation of extreme liberal wing to capture the limelight of the Democratic nomination for the 2020 American presidential election. If not else, passing one incentive to the other to the public as throwing bread to the masses, has the "hallmark" card of nationalism battling against the administration of a presidential tyrant that must confront, not only a COVID-19 pandemic spawned by a world health fiasco, but also besieged by spending cuts and extreme opposition on both ends to reshape the American landscape in their own image. If anything, else, normal doesn't define the American Democratic fringe, instead normality redefines itself in terms of a desperate corporate sector imposing discipline to contain an out of control party-delinquents hurrying to dominate the White House by falsely intruding into long-term economic interest.

To reshape American political history by bankrupting the U.S. Treasury with plummeting oil prices; calling on a return to a new normal (and in hopes of opening a political advantage for the Democratic Party).

But then and now, does a political tyrant, e.g., the Indonesian dictator President Suharto or the Iraqi president Saddam Hussein, pillage and plunder their own government to hide the incredulous crimes of a corporate model that can no longer achieve any sustainable implementation (even through the U.S. Supreme Court).

The edifice of war-crime is to cover up both deadly and destructive decision-making by all possible means -- to the magnitude, of ethnic cleansing, genocide, and/or regional biowarfare. And on all both ends, war-crime is being waged to drive a tyrant out of power and yet to cover up a tyrant to expose the Democrat's willingness to side with liberal ultra-nationalist extremism; to flip the balance of power to an extreme Democratic party-fringe that knows neither no moderation nor no bounds.

As not to incite and transform a pathological mass movement into totalitarian acts of pillage and plunder -- of what remains of U.S. constitutionality and the international rule of law.

www.ingramcontent.com/pod-product-compliance
Lightning Source LLC
Chambersburg PA
CBHW080505220526
45465CB00006B/2385